HEALING
AMERICA

HEALING
AMERICA

A Story Written to
African Americans for All People

A.W.

To order additional copies of this book, contact:
Xlibris Corporation
1-888-795-4274
www.Xlibris.com
Orders@Xlibris.com
113595

Introduction

America has a cancerous growth. It appears to be in remission. However, it will never be healed until the symptoms are identified, isolated and removed. Our daughter, JJ, came home from school one day when she was ten years old. She asked me "Daddy what is a nigger?" It turned out that the younger blond haired, blue eyed sister of one of her classmate friends had called her a nigger during their bus ride home.

During her school bus ride home in 1998 my daughter was exposed to the cancer that has taken the lives of many of our ancestors. The memories are fresh. I had not inoculated our daughter against this disease. Things are so much better in America. But the disease of racism is still here and will be here until its existence and the lingering effects of its horrible history is acknowledged and healed. The attempts to heal have been like trying to fill the Grand Canyon with a teaspoon.

Every reasonable person will agree that the victims of racism endure the worst humanity has to offer. History's accounts of the mental and physical mutilation of the victims of American racism are replete with atrocities that rival any evil that has been directed at any humans on the planet in the history of mankind.

While stationed in Germany In 1985 my wife and I along with other battalion staff officers and their mates had an opportunity to go through Check Point Charlie to go to East Berlin before the Wall came down. We visited a museum on the west side of the wall in West Berlin. There were lamp shades made of human skin. We saw a gun that had a human thigh bone for a stock. There were a number of other reminders of the terrible Holocaust.

During a visit to a German winery, I met and talked to a lady that went through the terrible ordeal. She told stories that would melt the hardest heart. She allowed me to see the identifying mark that was branded into her lower arm.

While attending a Regional Democratic Convention in Southeastern North Carolina a short time ago I met a Native American gentleman. We talked about a number of topics. One of those topics was the Trail of Tears. The forced death march was horrible.

I have talked to a number of people from various nationalities. Many of them had histories filled with pain. Across the board there have been instances where people have done horrible things to other people. However, what the American slaves, their descendants, American slave owners and their descendants experienced are unique.

American Slavery has served to prove that African Americans are some of the greatest people on the planet. I may be a bit biased on this point. When I consider what the American Negro has had to overcome I am amazed. We are expected to accept what has happened and just get over it. How does one get over such a horrible wrong when you live in a country that has not and will not acknowledge it as wrong?

America cannot acknowledge its legacy of wrong without enduring a great deal of pain. Those that endured and continue to endure often do not want to relive the pain of their ancestors or deal with the reality of the residual effects. Those that caused the pain do not want to acknowledge the atrocities of the pass and their undue benefits they enjoy.

We were three fifths of a person at one time. For this reason many of us did not believe we deserved more than the scraps of life we were forced to receive. Humans could feel good about the fact that they acquired much of their wealth on the backs of those creatures which were not human. It had to be OK because our great country said it was the way things had to be.

God has allowed us to come through a hurricane of social discord. He is waiting for us to realize that we are all His children. When humans can overcome feeling bad about what was and what they sometime do, we all can accept responsibility and move forward.

Regardless what side of the social and racial divide we Americans find ourselves, we must know we come from one beginning. We can go back to Adam or we can go back to Noah. For us to live up to what is best for all humanity, we must live up to what God would have us to do.

There are so many things in the African Americans' experience that make it clear that we more than any other people should envelop ourselves in what some would call the white man's religion. They say so because Christianity was used in many ways to keep us in bondage. However, what was meant for our bad was used for our good. We were taught the word so we would obey our masters and remain slaves.

The head knowledge of the Bible could and would have kept us in bondage until the end of creation. However, the words from Genesis 1 to Revelation last allowed us to know the Word. John 1:1 tells us that in the beginning was the Word . . . . John 1:14 explains that the Word became flesh and dwelt among us.

To keep us in bondage we were allowed to study the word. When 2 Timothy 2:15 says Study the Word to show yourself approved unto God . . . . While still in the shackles of slavery, our ancestors knew the Word. This Word is what allows all mankind to be free. Until we can reconcile that this is an incontrovertible truth we will all be slaves to a master called sin that rewards all its subjects with death.

We are to pattern our living after God. If He does not show partiality to any human (Acts 10:34 explains that God is not a respecter of persons), we humans cannot rightly be racist and please Him. The discussion of what is racism, prejudice, discrimination and the many other socially unacceptable behaviors are present based on the point of view of those doing the observing.

Webster will not be challenged or supported. I will share some events in the circles of the people who have influenced my life. From these events you can decide for yourself.

Losing Our Treasures

Our older African Americans are our living treasures. In many instances they have firsthand knowledge of the challenges and cruelties that we have had to overcome as a people. My cousin Lillian is one of these treasures.

Cousin Lillian was my late father's first cousin and his stepsister. My father's mother and her father were sisters and brothers. After my father's mother died and Cousin Lillian's father died, my father's father married Cousin Lillian's mother, Miss Annie Jane. My father's mother died in 1953. I was born in 1956. Miss Annie Jane was the only grandmother I ever knew.

Miss Annie Jane delivered most of the babies, both white and black in our community. I learned this fact long after she was dead. She died when I was a small child. Our people of hers and my grandfather's time were only one generation removed from slavery. Their parents' were slaves. Some of the devastating cruelty of slavery greatly influenced the relationships of the children of slavery.

We learn now that the slave master would mate together different slaves based on their physical attributes. This was done for economical reasons. In the master's attempt to produce a better worker, they planted in the African American family a germ that if left unchecked would destroy the most important foundation of our people. Even today we can see that much of our family values have been assaulted. But the connection to our past is what is influencing much of the actions of us as a people. To get into the psychology and the cause and effect of many of the slave tactics and their effects would create materials for many volumes. I would sum up by saying that slavery was a cause and we are suffering from the effects.

The slave had to be broken in order to be a useful piece of property. Beaten out of them was any sense of self-worth. An African based much of their worth on his or her heritage which was rooted in their family values. So to remove this obstacle to riches, the master systematically had to destroy the African American family. Many of the ways were overt. Some were subtle.

The master would have one slave beat a near kinsman. These beatings would sometime result in a beating to death. Imagine the horrors of watching your brother die. Multiply this horror when you consider that your brother died at your hand. Consider being forced out of bed to go tend the master's fields in the early morning while the master crawled into bed with your wife before your spot got cold. Imagine having your child torn from your arms and sold to never be seen or heard from again. Imagine the worst possible physical and emotional assault on the family of a race of people who held family as the foundation of their existence and you will have imagined the holocaust which is uniquely that of the African American.

I can remember as a young boy watching my grandfather (Poppa) sitting in a rocking chair on the porch of his old, small, tin top farm house reading the Bible. I can see the tears streaming down his face. I can hear him cry out; "*THE LORD HAS BROUGHT US FROM A LONG WAY*" *as* he wiped the tears with the white handkerchief that was his constant companion. Very often a white handkerchief was used by my grandfather to wipe away tears of joy and sometimes tears of sorrow.

I can imagine as he read his Bible and thought back over his 100 plus years of living he could recall much to be sad about. Being the son of slaves and the youngest of twelve children he embodied the sum total of the struggles of all who were before him in his biological and community family. I have been recently informed by a cousin who is researching our family tree that my grandfather was much older than we thought.

According to my older cousin, my father explained to him that my grandfather was well over a hundred when he died in 1973. This cousin shared information he explained my grandfather told him. My grandfather was a small child of about five year's old living in Waycross Georgia with his family when the slaves were freed. When they were freed they began to walk north.

As they walked north they kept mostly in the wooded areas for survival. Along this trek, different groups would settle in different areas. My grandfather and his family settled in the Town Creek, Brunswick County area of North Carolina. Poppa, the youngest of twelve, was not only the son of slaves, but he was also a slave.

Poppa was a proud man grounded in his Christian faith. The first pair of shoes he wore was a man's size seven. His earliest existence involved hard work. Poppa's life story is very much like all African American men of his generation. They did not have access to the opportunities afforded whites. They were forced to be weak, dossal, less than whole men. Their women were brutalized. The laws on the books did not allow them any legal recourse for the injustices that were a constant part of their lives. The weakness that was forced upon them served to make them stronger than those trying to make them weak. He depended on the Lord.

I believe Poppa understood **2 Corinthians 12:9 And he said unto me, My grace is sufficient for thee: for my strength is made perfect in weakness. Most gladly therefore will I rather glory in my infirmities, that the power of Christ may rest upon me.**

That is why; through his tears of pain and joy he could say "*the Lord has brought us a long way*". He lived through the knowledge of what his slave parents had to go through. The strength of God allowed him to live through being legally three fifths of a person. This same strength gave him the perseverance to wait on the Lord as our country recognized men like my Poppa and those that followed as whole men legally.

Before he died in October 1973, my grandfather saw from where the Lord had brought us. To endure the generational horrors placed upon the people of my Poppa's generation is almost beyond human comprehension. I believe that the fiber of my grandfather's character was fortified with what his parents and the generations before held onto from the land from which they were torn.

I can imagine that it was innately ingrained in some of our people the ability to be transported spiritually by a merciful God back to a time and place where family was the foundation of our culture. The spirit of our fore parents draws our collective spirits as a people together to support one another. Although, over the centuries of our bondage, the notion of family has been systematically attacked almost to the point of our lost of identity as a people, we have been blessed with the ability to overcome. There is a residual effect of our bondage that continues to threaten our families. The laws in place which are designed to support broken homes are also damaging our families. However, the family of God will be kept. The makeup of this family is designated by spirit. But race has been a tool to be used for division.

I believe that because of what our part of God's family has had to go through, we have been shown favor. We have been given extraordinary power. If it is true, as I believe, that He will put no more on us than we can bear, what people other than we could have endured what we have endured. There has been slavery long before America's brand of slavery. However, slavery in America was different. In no other instances, to my knowledge, were the slaves thought of as less than human. That was our plight and the residual effects of this phenomenon are with us today.

Our connection to God and the land of our beginning is what has and will continue to give us the strength to overcome. We are tied to our pass for our benefit. We are a peculiar people. We are brought to an understanding of the greatness of us as a people when we reflect on whose we are and from where we came. These connections will take us to greater heights. When we act in a way that does not reflect the greatness that is within us we do all of humanity a disservice.

I can hear in my heart from our ancestors telling us *"YOU WEREN'T RAISED LIKE THAT"* when we succumb to external pressures that would damage our families. These words come from a time back in Africa not on the American shores. We have to go back to the root of our existence to see what we are truly about. We should not rely on the words of those that would destroy us to define us. We have a strength that is a part of us.

There is a beacon of hope in each of us. This beacon shines in us even if miscegenation has diluted the blood that came from Africa to America. The strength of this blood is such that if a small portion of it were found in any of us, America deems us black or African American. The life of Africa that is in us connects us. We are a rich people from a rich land.

When I think of our people, I see parallels to the plight of the children of Israel. The difficulties they encountered are documented. However, much of what we went through is not documented on paper. Our struggle is documented on the backs and in the hearts and minds of our people.

What my grandfather and others of his generation went through is a part of a river of tears that flows down from those of our people that suffered before them. That river flows through my father's generation, my generation and all the generations that follow.

The Negro working on the plantation had hopes and dreams of crossing this river to freedom. They placed this desire in the hearts of their children and the generations that came after them. Many only crossed the river when they entered into the freedom of death.

This imagery is passed down to and through us. The connection to our beginning is passed to us through the blood. There is a drawing on each of us to revel in the love that was planted in us in Africa. Although the weeds of discourse have tried to strangle the nature of our people from us, we each still have seeds of the love that has been transplanted in the hearts of each us from when our home was Africa.

We have been a weary people in a strange land. But thanks be to God we can now say that we are African Americans. Although the politics of the day have not quite caught up to where it should be, we can say it is moving in the right direction. All humanity must know that we all come from the same source. When this is an accepted reality, we can then say as the Negro spiritual, the phrase Dr. Mr. Luther King, Jr. used to instill hope in all of America which is "Free At Last Free At Last, Thank God All Mighty I Am Free At Last".

Freedom is not possible unless all of humanity is free. We are our brothers' keeper. When humanity comes to grips with the fact that the chain of humanity is only as strong as its weakest link, we will all be free. It starts in the biological and immediate family. Each family is a link in the chain of humanity. We must ensure that each is strong regardless of national origin to ensure that all are strong.

The responsibility belongs to individual families to strengthen their link. The strength of one should not be a threat to another. If we all get about the business of strengthening our own families we can be a help to other families.

Although the desire to strengthen our families has been twisted within our African American culture over the centuries, it was not so for our people before Plymouth Rock landed on us, (to coin a phrase from Malcolm X). Family value was one of the things that had to be beaten out us to make us useful slaves. The family value had to be replaced with the "Crab Syndrome" to make us useful. As long as we tried to keep each other down we could not see who was keeping us all down.

We brought no crabs from Africa. We as a people were constantly fed on a diet of mistrust. But the sweet taste of family was forever on the minds of many of us. To those who have developed a taste for this crab THAT WILL EVENTUALLY DESTROY US, we must move back to the healthy diet of family values.

I am blessed. Because growing up in the poverty resulting from the lack of material things; I was blessed in the riches of family love. What I saw in the elders of my community had to be from what travelled in our ancestors from Africa. That thing is a love of family. The last living family member of my father's from his generation is a testament to what could not be beaten out of us in our generations before us.

Cousin Lillian is that person. She and my father were extremely close. But she and my mother were even closer. One of the reasons I think that Cousin Lillian and my father were so close was because they shared the same birth month. Cousin Lillian was born May 26, 1922. My father was born May 23, 1911. Sharing a birth month was such a small part of their relationship. My father and mother were Godparents to her third oldest child. The depth of their love could not be measured.

That which was carried in the hearts of those that survived the murderous voyage from Africa is what knitted their hearts together. When I talk to Cousin Lillian today, her eyes well up as she recalls and shares many of the trials and tribulations that they had to endure. The list is too long to be contained within the covers of this writing. Some of the stories she tells with a bit of humor. I believe the humor is for my sake as well as hers. The brutality and inhumanity of man toward man is too much to bear.

She tells the stories with humor so as to dampen the pain of reliving the horror. As I try to see in her far off almost glazed over eyes to detect the pain, I see it very clearly. However, a smile on her face is a hedge around me so I do not feel the pain that is contained in her stories.

There are many movies and writings that recount the nature of the brutality our people endured. But they only share the immediate physical and emotional pain. I have not watched one of these movies that follow the trail of sorrow over the generations. The emotional devastation of the beating, lynching, burning, raping, and many forms of psychological depravity will never be adequately measured or healed. If we had gotten the forty acres and a mule it may have helped.

Our treasures are leaving. They are taking the hard earned wisdom and knowledge they have with them. We all would benefit from knowing what they know. So instead of highlighting all the terrible things that have happened, let us concentrate on how we as a people have overcome. Let us not forget our holocaust. But let us keep it in our rear view mirror as we look forward to a bright future.

Let us keep in front of us all the positives from our past and present. The most important positive from our past is our seniors. The wisdom they have will serve us well in our future. How well we take care of our treasures is a measure of how we advance as a people. Cousin Lillian is one of the living treasures our family has today.

Cousin Lillian, who will be 90 May 23, 2012, maintains her house. She cooks and cleans and keeps a hearty appetite. She also maintains a garden. She still drives. Although she laments the fact that because of her age she has a provisional license that only allows her to drive a 50 mile radius from her home. This draw back may hamper the Multilevel Marketing Business she has recently started. However, knowing her it will not stop her.

She recently became the last of my father's cousin of my father's generation. Her 96 year old sister, Cousin Bertha, recently died. Another treasure is gone.

We have so far to go. Our treasures will finance our journey with the currency of wisdom and love. Bless the eldest person in your family. Cousin Lillian is the last on my father's side.

My mother's baby sister, Aunt Olivia or Aunt Livy Ann or Aunt Lil as we call her is the last on my mother's side. Aunt Lil turned 88 years old January 13, 2012. Whenever someone asks her how she is feeling, her response is usually, "Pretty Good for A Old Plug". When I was a child growing up, Aunt Lil was my favorite aunt. Through the dip of snuff that is her constant companion, she has a heart of laughter. It seems as though almost every other statement she makes is accompanied by laughter.

There have been a number of harsh realities in her life. She shares them in a matter of fact manner with no apparent ill will. She was married to my daddy's first cousin who looked almost white. She told with humor how her in-laws thought she was to dark for him. I guess after seven children they got the message.

Even within our community there is no secret that there was and maybe still is some prejudices based on skin tone. I am not a psychiatrist. However, I believe there is an obvious link between what happened in slavery to how we as a people interact with each other. Even in our childhood sayings the slavery connection is easily seen.

"ENIE MEANIE MINIE MOE CATCH A "N WORD" BY THE TOE, IF HE HOLLA LET HIM GO"
"IF YOU WHITE YOU RIGHT, IF YOU BLACK STAY BACK"

It is amazing what stays with you over the years. At the age of about five years old, I remember an older cousin, explaining to me why I should use tiger instead of "n word" when making a choice by chance. The lesson stuck. Today I find it distasteful to use and to hear the "n word".

Maybe it is my ignorance that causes me to be offended by a mere word. That same ignorance is probably what makes me feel uneasy when I see the Confederate flag. But is it my ignorance or my enlighten understanding.

"Sticks and stones may break my bones. But words will never hurt me." I recall hearing myself recite this saying in response to hurtful words that had been hurled at me. Saying these words would sometimes fend off a verbal attack. But I cannot recall them easing the pain or diminishing the power of poison filled words. There is life and death in the tongue.

Our world and all creation were spoken into existence except man. It is taught in the Christian faith that all creation occurred in six days. There is power in the Word. Words have histories that make them either pleasant or painful. As an African American, everything about the n'word is painful to me.

When I hear the word I think of my ancestors being treated like animals. I can see the little African American children being fed in troughs as if they were like the other animals on the plantation. I can hear and see the slave master running the African American male slave out of his marriage bed to the fields before sun up so he could witness the sunrise while defiling the mate of the slave. My imagination can feel the whip come down across my mental back like the whip that split the flesh of my ancestors at the whim of the master. The word brings home the stinging irony of laws that protected the master if he killed an African American slave in the process of correcting them. You had a right to do as you please with your property.

In the year 2012 while watching a debate about slavery on television, I was mystified by one of the young white gentlemen who defended the rights of the slave master by explaining with much conviction that a person had the right to do as they pleased with their property.

Yes, the law of the land said that our ancestors were less than human and could rightly be treated as property. Who in 2012 and beyond believe and will believe that this was a just law? Unfortunately, much of the rhetoric spewed by many of the American hate groups today would say that this was a just law. To believe anything else would force them to face the cold hard facts that their ancestors were the ones that were less than humans for the way they treated other humans.

The n'word was part of the pathology that gave comfort to those who held to the notion that we African Americans were less than humans. Why would any human seek to destroy a part of themselves? We are all part of humanity. When any person tears down a part of humanity, they are also tearing down the whole of which they are a part.

Why use words that aid in the destruction of us all. Similarly, why hold in high esteem symbols that are equally as divisive when considering the well being of all of humanity? A symbol that causes most thinking African

Americans and other enlightened Americans to cringe is the Confederate Flag.

As in the case of most symbols, the actual flag itself is neutral until the history is attached. How many Jewish people over the age of fifty would ever drive a Volkswagen (VW-people's wagon)? I do not think any of the descendants of those who went to the German death camps would be caught dead in a Volkswagen.

The Volkswagen vehicles are wonderfully made according to all the awards they have received over the years. But the history that attaches them to Hitler makes the VW offensive to many Jewish people and those that empathize with their holocaust.

Most people would like to separate themselves from those things that bring back bad memories. I am not surprised that Jewish people would not want the memories associated with the VW.

Many Africa Americans view the Confederate Flag as a symbol of slavery and the oppression and bigotry that was spawned by slavery. This flag represents a dark part of our American History. There are those that would say it is a matter of pride. How does one find pride in a symbol that represents the devastation of a people?

As distasteful as it is, I would defend any person's right to display the Confederate Flag. Our history is linked to it. When we see it, we should be encouraged by how far we and our country have come. The Lord has brought us a mighty long ways. However, we have a long way to go.

Those symbols of what was our destruction can now be viewed as a testament to the strength of us as a people for what we have had to overcome. There is a slave auction square on Hay Street in Fayetteville, North Carolina. A number of years ago there was a movement to have this symbol of shame demolished. Wiser heads prevailed. The last time I visited the area this symbol was still there. I hope it stays there.

I was one of those folks who thought it should be removed because of all of the painful memories. Now I believe it should be there forever because of all of the painful memories. We must not forget. We should not hold the memories as fuel for a justified anger. We should hold on to these memories to fortify our gratitude to an awesome God. For it is only by the grace of God that we as a people have come as far as we have.

2 Chronicles 7:14: If my people, which are called by my name, shall humble themselves, and pray, and seek my face, and turn from their wicked ways; then will I hear from heaven, and will forgive their sin, and will heal their land.

Every descendant of slaves has a similar story to tell. There is nothing new under the sun. Many of our stories are linked to times long passed.

Egypt was a land of bondage for God's children. America was also a land of bondage for God's children. There was a reason for the Egypt experience. There was a reason for the American experience. His ways are not our ways. However, for those who would trust, believe and keep His commandments there is a more abundant life for us.

The influence of the many generations that came before us is evident today. The attitudes of the descendants of the oppressed and the oppressors have been shaped by what has been passed down through the generations.

The descendants of the oppressors are given the edge in wealth because of generational prosperity that has been passed down. If you tell someone something long enough they may eventually start to believe it. The oppressors have taught that they and those that look like them were better. They had the force of law behind them. If they did not inherit wealth, they still inherited opportunity. This by virtue of the fact they were always thought of as human.

The descendants of the oppressed are given the edge in intestinal fortitude with the ability to endure and overcome. It is only the favor of God that has allowed us to move from the Slave House to the White House. We must not forget the mountains of challenges that have been placed before us. We must hold on to the truth of the obstacles. We must use the memories as stepping stones to higher heights for all of humanity. Woven within the fabric of our history are countless stories.

Our wise elders have rich experiences that can benefit us all. They are truly our treasures. Each of them has many stories that would serve us all well. At my tender age of fifty six I am at the crossroads of an intellectual divide. I am not yet old enough to have inherited the wisdom that would come with time. However, I am too old to be forgiven for mistakes due to youth. Keeping these facts in mind, allow me to tell my story. I hope I can come close to giving proper acknowledgement and gratitude to our elders for their wisdom.

My Story

My story is similar to any descendant of slaves. I have so many things for which I am grateful. Working at a paper mill in North Carolina, gives me reason to be extremely grateful. Besides the wages I have earned, since I came to work here April 15, 1996, I have received a lesson for life.

I have been able to experience firsthand a portion of what my father and his father as well as other Negros in the south had to endure during their lifetimes. My grandfather, John, was born into slavery around 1860 the youngest of twelve children. My father, Andrew was born May 23, 1911. Daddy was the third oldest of nine boys. My father had no sisters.

My father and grandfather were both deacons at Christian Hope Christian Church. I believe their relationship with God is what sustained them until their deaths. My grandfather died in 1973. My father died in 1995. I was born in 1956 the youngest of my father's 8 children. There were 3 girls and five boys. I grew up believing I was the youngest of 7 children, 5 boys and two girls. After my mother's death in 1987 I learned that I had an older half sister.

I learned from my older sisters and brothers and by my own experiences that we children were sheltered from much by our parents and older relatives. I remember as a young child accompanying my Aunt Hazel to Wilmington. At the age of four going on five, I had not yet been taught that Negros and Whites did not mix. So I was confused when we went to a restaurant and could not go in the front door. We went around to the back and these wonderful Negro ladies welcomed us in the kitchen. Maybe they knew my aunt. Maybe they understood what I had not yet learned.

My experiences and those of others at the Paper Mill Plantation remind me of times of my childhood. I have had a chance to relive lessons I had to learn as a child. Fortunately, the grace of God and the teachings of my childhood have given me the strength to endure.

Since its beginning in the 1950s and its purchase in 1996 the Paper Mill has made some changes. However, based on some of the conversations I have had with coworkers who have worked there many more years than I, the different administrations have held onto some distasteful southern traditions. These traditions are not unique to our Paper Mill. As I share my experiences and those of other workers, the influences of the **"Old South"** will be evident.

In my short 56 years I have done a lot of living. I was blessed to have parents that believed in love and moral discipline. They lived the life before us. They instilled in me, by their work ethic and sacrifices for their children, a desire to please them. I learned the Lord's Prayer before I learned how to spell my name. They equipped me with the ability to deal with the struggles of life. They also raised me to believe I could accomplish anything as long as I put God first.

I attribute having been: an honor graduate from High School, a football player at State College, survived the divorce from my first wife, been a captain in the US Army, an honor graduate from another University and survived the murder of my oldest brother and the death of my parents to what they instilled in me. Even though the challenges have been great since I have been employed at the Paper Mill Plantation, what my parents gave me has been enough to sustain me.

My brother, James was murdered in May 1985 at the age of 45, while I was serving as the Adjutant for of an Engineer Battalion in Germany. My brother lived a tortured life as a result of his battle with alcohol. When I was about 15, James moved back home from Connecticut to live with my parents and me. James, along with my other brothers and sisters, Willie, Curtis, Tim, Glenda and Evelena had moved north for opportunities that were not available to Negroes in the south at the time. I assumed James' beautiful wife, who moved to Connecticut from Mississippi, chose to raise their two young boys and daughter alone rather than allow her entire family to become a causality of the war with alcohol, in which James was engaged.

From the time James moved home until I left for college, he and I were estranged because of the person he became when he was drinking. When James "Sugar Boy" was not drinking he lived up to his nickname. He was a wonderful, fun loving person to be around when he was not drinking. But when he was drinking, he became verbally abusive. I could deal with it for myself because he did not go too far with me. However, I could not deal with his foul language when it came to our parents. The only time I ever raised my hand to my brother was when he used foul language toward my parents. Because of this incident and other issues, James and I were at odds from about 1971 until shortly before his death in 1985. I believe it was the prayers and faith of my parents that allowed James and me to make up before he was murdered.

In April 1985 we officers from the Engineer Battalion, flew from, Germany to Cape Cod for a weekend field exercise. We were a float bridge battalion. It was a paper exercise conducted on a hard site (buildings with running water and electricity). After the exercise was over I requested leave to spend a week at home before going back to Germany. I was hoping to reconcile my differences with my brother.

I flew into Wilmington. I do not remember who came to the airport to pick me up and take me 18 or so miles home. I just remember feeling an urgency to find my brother. The urgency to see my brother was odd. I would have thought that my desire to see my future wife, Dalphaine, would have overshadowed my desire to see my brother. However, it did not. When I got home I could not find James. I was told that he was in the Oaks at the Hospital. The Oaks is a place where people are committed or commit themselves to reestablish a connection with reality. To say the least, I was concerned.

I went to the Oaks to see James. It turned out he was using the Oaks to help him in his war against alcoholism. The confinement seemed to be doing him good. We cried and slobbered together as we became reunited as brothers. This was the first time I remember us saying we loved each other. I think our visit lasted for over an hour. I left with a huge wait lifted off my shoulders. The big brother I once thought so much of as a kid was coming back. This was one of the happiest days of my life.

I visited my future wife and the rest of my family and friends before leaving to go back to Germany. When the plane landed I continued to float on a cloud of happiness. Shortly after returning, things just kept getting better. A lieutenant in the Battalion was leaving Germany and wanted someone to take over the least to his apartment. I was living in the Bachelor Officers Quarters (BOQ) at the time in Heidelberg. The BOQ was about a 15 minute drive from my office. The apartment on the economy (German civilian population) was less than a 15 minute walk from my office. The weekend after I returned from the States, I was gleefully finishing my move into my furnished fourth floor apartment. The German landlord provided everything except the clothes I wore and my TV. I paid rent into a bank account. I think I called Dalphaine that weekend and asked her if she was ready to get married. She said yes. I knew that when I got transferred back to the States in about a year we would be getting married.

Monday, I walked to work almost floating. Happiness is an understatement when used to describe how I felt on this beautiful day. I got to work a few minutes before the start of the duty day. I was not fazed by the somber faces as I entered the Battalion Headquarters building. This huge "L" shaped building was about as big as a football field. I went through the large doors at the main entrance which were almost directly across from my office (personnel/S1 section). If you turned right and went about 20 feet the Sergeant Major's office was on the left. If you went another 20 feet or so the Battalion Commander's office was on the left and straight ahead. The office of his secretary was at the very end of the building. The Battalion Executive Officer's office was to the right of the Battalion Commander Secretary's office.

If you turned left when you came into those big doors and went about 20 feet, on the left was the S4 section. If you kept going in this direction about 40 feet you would come to a right turn that gave the building its "L" shape. In the "L" were the offices of the German Unit that fell under our Battalion. This unit was like a separate company in that they took care of all their personnel actions independent of us. They operated in support of us. In comparison to the US Army this Unit would be somewhere between a National Guard unit and a Regular Army unit. This was an all German unit. Some of the men in this unit had held the same job for over 30 years. It showed in the precision way they put the bridge sections together on the water during training exercises. My counterpart in this unit was my late dear friend Ludwig. Ludwig was a Captain also. We called each other brother because that is the way we felt about each other. Ludwig is survived by his beautiful wife Rashida from Kenya and her handsome son and beautiful daughter.

After you made the hard right and go about 50 feet you would be at the entrance to the tavern on the right. Somewhere in the building were the Communications Section and the Intelligence Section. There was also a downstairs/basement to this building.

Inside the "L" and outside the building, detached from the Headquarters building was the dining hall. This facility was run by the Germans. They did a great job. The food was great. It took me some time to get use to the large breakfasts, medium lunches and light dinners. It makes sense to eat this way. But I was use too the opposite. I did adjust.

There were a number of nuances that made the building and the relationship between the units special. However, to get back on point let me return to the Monday morning after I completed my move into my apartment among the German nationals.

I came to work that morning full of glee. As I walked through the big front doors, my assistant met me before I could get in my office. He seemed to be almost in tears as he told me that the "XO" (Executive Officer) wanted to see me in his office. This was nothing unusual, in light of the fact that we were deactivating the battalion. In his capacity as the Executive Officer, he would often be updated on our progress or give guidance.

As soon as my assistant delivered the message I went into my office and grabbed a note pad. I cheerfully headed down the hall to the XO's office. The looks I was getting as I went to his office seemed a little strange. But nothing could get me down. At that moment my life was sunshine and rainbows.

I got to the XO's door and peered through the translucent glass as I had done on many other occasions. Everything seemed normal until I saw the figure behind the desk get up just before I knocked on the door. Usually, I would knock on the door and he would say come in while sitting behind his large imposing desk. In the few seconds it took him to walk from his desk across the distance of his large office I could not wrap my mind around what was happening.

He opened his door for me to come in. I could not recall him ever doing that for me as he beckoned me to enter. At this point I was still floating on a cloud of happiness. So, I came in with a big smile ready for anything or at least I thought I was. I was walking with him back to his desk as he paused and said with a solemn almost tearful voice, Captain Jenkins; I am sorry to inform you, we received a Red Cross . . . . When the words Red Cross fell from his lips, I immediately threw my pad across his office as I screamed James and very unprofessionally broke down and started to cry. Very quickly I regained my composer. After all I was a Captain in the United States Army.

I do not remember very much after the XO delivered the message. It seemed as if he was talking to me from a great distance as he explained that the Red Cross and the Battalion Headquarters had been trying to get up with me over the weekend. I think I may have told him that I had moved. I am not sure. Somehow I got packed and wound up at the airport waiting to get an emergency flight home. The only thing I remember about the waiting at the airport is someone calling me to the desk for the next flight.

When I got to the desk they gave me my last four of my social security number but it was not me for whom they were looking. I am not sure this was a real memory. But it seems real to me.

Somehow I boarded the plane, made the eight hour flight, changed planes, landed at the Wilmington airport and found myself standing beside James' bed in the hospital. I only have clear recall of coming to work, receiving a message from my assistant, going to the XO's office, being at the airport in Germany and then being beside my brother's bed.

I think the decision was made to turn off his life support after I arrived. I think I died a little that day. Why am I shedding tears as I write this? After I walked out of my brother's room, I met the detective that was investigating the case. He explained that they had the person in custody. I asked the detective if I could see him. He said no in a tone that led me to believe he thought I wanted to do this person harm. I do not think that was my motive at all. I just wanted to know why. I was still in a daze. For years and even today I am still troubled by my brother's death. I did not go to the gentleman's trial who murdered James. So, I did not get the specifics of what happened or the why.

For forty five days I was home on leave. It was as though I was someone else doing the things I was doing. It was as if I was observing a stranger. I know I went to my brother's funeral. But during my leave and even today I cannot recall any of the details. I have visited the grave of my oldest brother. I pray the torture James endured in life is gone forever.

My time home was full of pain and joy. I experienced the pain of my brother's funeral. I experienced the joy of marrying Dalphaine. I was mostly on automatic during this time. Dalphaine was at Jacksonville, finishing her Marine training. It was a challenge to get things in order so my bride could travel back to Germany with me. There were a few obstacles we had to overcome. She had to finish her Marine Basic Training. We had to get her placed on Inactive Reserves. We had to get her birth certificate. We had to get her passport. A number of other things had to be done. However, it was all worth it. Working to lay the foundation for my new life with my new wife helped ease the pain of losing my brother.

I was determined to get started on the right foot. So, a short time after my brother's funeral, I went to work making arrangements to take my bride back to Germany with me. Since Dalphaine was in Jacksonville training, she could not be with me as I worked to complete my mission. I thought it was a formality. None the less, I thought it was right to ask Dalphaine's father for her hand in marriage.

I wanted to do things right this time. I did not want to have the outcome of other relationships and what I had in my first marriage to happen again. After almost six years of marriage, my first wife had enough of the jerk that was me. As a young First Lieutenant I sat in the back row of the Wake County, court room, in my class "A" uniform, as I listened to my wife tell a judge the reasons she was divorcing me. At 9:45am on Thursday September 2, 1982 our divorce became final. Before she got out of the witness chair, I walked outside the courtroom and waited.

I stood in the hallway outside the courtroom trying to muster all the military bearing I could. In the few minutes I waited for her to come from the courtroom, I think my married life flashed before my eyes. I could not imagine any battle field injury that could cause the pain that I was feeling. However, by the time she exited the courtroom she found in me a pillar of strength. I asked her for a moment of her time. The young lady that was with her excused herself so we could talk.

Our conversation was brief and one-sided. I presented her an envelope filled with every picture I had of her. I then said *"I WILL NEVER SEE YOU AGAIN IN THIS LIFETIME"*. I turned crisply and marched out of her presence. Even though we lived in the same town for about two more years after our divorce, I never saw her.

After a reasonable mourning period, after my divorce, I started being an unrestricted philanderer. I later located a high school girlfriend, who lived in New Haven Connecticut. I went to Connecticut to visit family with the additional intention of reigniting the flame of a high school sweetheart. I was cool as a cucumber. After a brief visit with my relatives I made a bee-line to the home of Olivia. I went flying in on the wings of hope for a new life. How was I to know that I would be shot down in flames?

It seemed that some memories were still fresh. Olivia was a gracious hostess. We were all laughter and cheer in our conversation. I never did get a chance to suggest that we might try a relationship again. All I could do the whole time I was there was listening at how wonderful her man, Jeff, was. *"Jeff and I did this . . . Jeff did this . . . I did this for Jeff . . . I am so in love with Jeff . . ."* Why would she want to be with the high school sweetheart that stopped seeing her to be with the woman who later became his wife? The divorce not only damaged my heart, it also damaged my head.

After getting over the sting, I was genuinely happy for Olivia. I drove back to Raleigh with my tail between my legs. For the next few weeks I was like a ship without a rudder. I did manage to go to work and function at a minimal level of competency. I was the only military person assigned to my office at the time. So, the scrutiny was a lot less than it could have been. I was a First Lieutenant at the time.

The late Hubert F. Baumgartner, who was a GS12, was my boss and good friend. I felt very close to everyone in the office. Everyone in the office was professional engineers except me. I was a Combat Engineer Officer; 21J.There was an air of professionalism mixed with friendship in this office that made going to work a joy. For this reason I thank Linda, Burt, Ray and later Ellen. Linda and her husband Jim took me to the circus during my time of mourning over my divorce. They will never know what this meant to me. I was a regular at Hubert's home. In the midst of a painful situation, God put human angels around me to make it bearable.

There was a hole in my soul. I missed being married. The void was engulfing me. The many nights I rode a bicycle through the streets of Raleigh I had time to think. I blocked my "X" from my mind. I needed someone to do more than lust after. I needed someone to love.

During one of my late night bike rides my mind took me to a happier time in my life. What female company did I enjoy? I remembered when my friends Willie, Sue, Elizabeth and I hung out together. We were the best of friends. Willie and Sue became romantic. Elizabeth and I were friends beyond friendship. We would start talking in the early evening and talk until the wee hours of the morning.

I needed that kind of friendship again. I located Elizabeth in New York City. For the next six months I put thirty five thousand miles on my new 1982 Chevrolet Cavalier going back and forth from Raleigh, North Carolina to New York, New York. I would leave Friday evening after work and drive the ten hours to see Elizabeth. I would leave Sunday evening and come home. I thought Elizabeth was the answer to my prayers. She was my dream come true. However, I turned out to be a nightmare for her. We became engaged to be married. Things were going well until Ray invited me to a cookout he and his wife Sheila were having. I went because Ray was a coworker and a friend.

Sheila introduced me to her coworker Deidra. Deidra gave me her phone number. I did not call her for a long time. I was engaged to Elizabeth. The person I was before was no more. So, I did not call right away. I do not remember if she called me or I called her. Somehow we got together. We got to know each other. I was still a jerk. After knowing Deidra, I called Elizabeth and saved her from a jerk like me. How could I have loved more than one woman at a time? Meeting Deidra, an older woman, who lived in the same town, gave me something to think about. She had a son, Tryvon, who made me happier than I had been in a long time. I felt the joy of being a father figure. He was a great kid. I am only about 15 years older than Tryvon. I enjoyed every moment I spent with him. Before I got transferred to Germany, Deidra and I realized that she was not going with me. I asked if I could take Tryvon with me. I wanted to adopt him. I am sorry my split with his mother caused a split between us. Understandably, she was not going to let her son go to Germany with me. It seemed as if I was striking out in all my relationships.

Another older lady friend, with whom I had a brief fling, told me that my "X" had ruined me for any other woman. I thought about all these things as I went from woman to woman trying to establish a meaningful relationship. But all I knew was that women who loved me wound up getting hurt. Hurting anyone, especially women, was not something I wanted to do. I figured I was not good for anybody.

My hyper-physical needs probably stemmed from being molested as a preschool child. It has been over 50 years and the images still haunt me. But that is no excuse for hurting someone else. I am very fortunate that my parents taught me about the Power, Goodness and Mercy of God as a small child. This knowledge is what has kept me through all the years. I wander from the right path every now and then. I thank them for the teachings that give me knowledge of the way back.

I do regret that when I do fall from the way that I cause pain to those that are in my wake. I pray now that those of you whom I have caused harm of any kind that you will forgive me. The hurt that I have caused has come back to me. I do not say this to justify my actions or inaction when action was necessary. I just state it as a point of fact.

My mission in life now is to put into practice the tried and true Christian teachings I received as a child. These teachings are the moral compass that allows me to have peace of mind when I know I am going in the right direction. It also causes an inner pain after I have gone astray. Unfortunately, momentary physical pleasures usually precede the inner pain of conscience. I am grateful for those teachings that remind me of the love, grace and mercy of my Lord and Savior Jesus Christ. This is needed to be said at this point so you and I can better know the person you are reading about. Life is a joy when we remember Romans 8:28 And we know that all things work together for good to them that love God, to them who are the called according to *His* purpose.

It comes to mind a conversation I had with elderly women from my community when I was a much younger man. These ladies were cousins from my parent's generation. People from my parent's generation made it a practice of visiting each other. So, it was not unusual to find a number of cousins gathered together at a home just enjoying each other's company. The women would be in the house and the men would be outside or grouped somewhere away from the women. Dr. Phil or Oprah had nothing on these people. The community is what helped a lot of Negros deal with what was going on outside and sometimes inside their homes.

On this one occasion the ladies were finding great sport in taking turn asking me personal and sometimes embarrassing questions. It was all good natured. They all had a good laugh, usually at the expense of the target of their questions. It just happened to be my turn on this particular day. After they saw that I was a little reluctant to give them any answers of substance, one commented "He thinks we are being nosy." I saw the direction the questions were about to go. The grilling I had gotten up to this point was nothing compared to what I was going to get. I had seen it happen to other young men. It was almost like a rite of passage into manhood. As they were marshalling their intellectual forces to put on an impressive assault on my level of comfort, I countered with a respectful two line assault that gave me a chance to retreat to safety. I explained to the apparent leader of this group of five elderly women: *"My life is an open book. I will tell you anything I want you to know."* Before they had a chance to challenge or think about what I said, I retreated to an area of safety away from their gaze.

Many wonderful encounters like this one was part of what influenced my development. I knew all their questions were part of their good natured fun. They forced us young men to learn to think on our feet. But they never tolerated any hint of disrespect. Every person of our parent's generation was like another parent with all the privileges afforded that position. The village did raise the children of my generation.

So, I do not have a good excuse for why I went off the right path so often in my life. My strongest weakness in my life has been women. I won't go through all the different conversations I had with myself in my attempts to diagnose my condition. I thank God for His mercy.

As my daughter, "JJ", would tell me, get back on point. These and so many other influences in my life are what has guided and continue to guide me on this road of life. The many women, sports, military, prison guard, self-employed, seen and unseen forces have brought me to this juncture in my life. They are the foundation on which I stand as I deal with my present employer, Paper Mill. By the time I write this book I may not be employed at the plantation. Some may say that plantation is too strong a word in my characterization of this Mill. After reading my experiences and the experiences shared with me by others, you be the judge.

As you read this I ask you to keep in mind a simple question. What is your dignity worth? Looking back over my life, I realize I have had to deal with this question more times than I care to count.

While I was struggling with taking care of my family, my beautiful wife found an ad for employment at the Paper Mill in the newspaper. At that time I did not think about the impact my stress was having on her. About eight years earlier, after two years of the National Guard and six years of the active Army, I tried to resign my commission. I had given up my dream of retiring as an army officer and teaching. I was suffering. I was bouncing around. I did not finish school as I had planned immediately after I left the army. I worked at a prison for about six of the most frustrating years of my life. I became self/unemployed. I was miserable. In retrospect, I know my wife suffered like I did. I took her advice and applied for a job at the Paper Mill. You would think I was trying to get a job at the Pentagon. Paper Mill was going through the transition of turning over ownership. The process of getting hired is worth noting.

All applicants had to go to the Employment Security Office in Whiteville to fill out an application. In order to get an application to fill out, one had to pass a basic reading and math test. A number of potential employees were weeded out by the test. Even with this process, there were still over seven thousand applicants for the few jobs that were available.

Those of us that were fortunate to pass the test were informed that we had to go to a two week course to get past the next step. This course was taught at night at a Middle School. Our compensation for attending these classes was a chance to work at the Paper Mill. I looked at this opportunity as another and at my age, forty, maybe my last chance to be made whole. I still am not sure exactly what they were looking for in the class. I just knew I had to be noticed in a positive way. This need to exceed and excel became more urgent with me when during one of the class breaks the instructor explained that this was the company's first hiring of this sort in eight years. He went on to explain that employment was going to be done in small staggered groups. All I knew was that I had to be in the first group.

I looked for ways to stand out. I was the classic try and answer all questions person. I hoped I did not offend anyone. However, I was thinking about my wife and two small children. So when the instructor asked the class what a word meant and no one knew the answer, including me, I saw an opportunity. I figured he would ask for the meaning of this word the next night. So I made it a point to find the definition of this word before I came to class the following night. Sure enough, at the beginning of class, he asked the definition of this word. Nobody knew the answer except you know who. The word was ergonomics. **Ergonomics (or human factors) is the scientific discipline concerned with the understanding of interactions among humans and other elements of a system, and the profession that applies theory, principles, data and methods to design in order to optimize human well-being and overall system performance.** I thought this was a good start. However, I could not take any chances. I was dealing with the lives of my loved ones.

We were told that at the end of the two week course there would be a test. I felt I was ready for whatever was thrown at me. But this was not enough for me. On the day we were going to take the test, I racked my brain to see how I could be noticed positively. I believe that God heard my prayers throughout this entire process. On the night of the test I wore a three piece suit to class. I was taking no prisoners. I took the test and felt pretty good as I left.

But you know when God starts blessing the devil starts messing. One of the instructors, who was also in Human Resources for the Paper Mill called me at home and explained in a slow monotone; **"Mr. Jenkins, we would like to hire you. However, you have a felony breaking and entering bench warrant out for your arrest."** After I picked my jaw up off the floor, I explained that there was nothing to it. He said I would have to get this matter straighten out before they could offer me a job.

After I got off the phone, I called the prison where I used to work (worst job I ever had). I figured that one of the inmates got a hold of my personal information and used my identity. After calls to the sheriff's department and a lot of leg work, I got this matter resolved. I got past this hurdle. I took paperwork to the mill confirming that I was not a **"FELON"**. After this matter was cleared up, they offered me and the rest of the first seven hires a job. This was contingent on whether we past a few physical tests.

Apparently I did OK. I was called a few days later and told to go take a urinalysis. After they got the results of the urinalysis, I got a call to schedule an interview. I came to the mill for this final interview. I sit before a panel of five people. HR, Hourly and Supervision were well represented. The interview probably lasted only about 20 minutes. But it seemed like hours. There were many different types of questions asked from all the members on the panel. However, I can only remember one question because of the answer I gave.

Someone asked me, how often were you absent from your former job? I could only think of the prison. But that is where my thinking stopped. I answered immediately, **"EVERY CHANCE I GOT".** The stunned look on their faces let me know that I had some **"SPLAINNING TO DO."** I explained to the panel that for six years I hated every minute I worked at the prison. So, every legitimate time I could be off I took it. Apparently this answer was acceptable because I was offered a job. I was among the first new hires. They gave me a start date, April 15, 1996.

Understanding what was available was now my objective. Watch as well as pray was and is my way of operating. History was against me. Fallout from the "Old South" was and is present at work. The stories about the actions of some of the ancestors of some of my coworkers are unbelievable.

The first story that comes to mind is about the events surrounding the assassination of Dr. Martin Luther King, Jr.. Most of the flags in America were to be flown at half staff to recognize the death of Dr. King. The administration of the Paper Mill, at the time, decided that they would fly Old Glory at half staff. Apparently this intent angered some of the workers at the Paper Mill.

I was told that leaders of the Union went to the Mill Manager to make their case against the intention to honor Dr. King. They gave the Mill Manager an ultimatum. It was said that they explained to the Mill Manager that if the flag was flown at half staff the Paper Mill would not make any paper. The Mill Manager had a counter offer.

The Mill Manager explained to this Union Committee that for every minute the machines were down that the union would be charged with the financial loss. These union representatives consulted their union lawyer. Because they believed that the Mill Manager's counter threat was unenforceable.

According to some of the blacks that were willing to talk about it, the union lawyer had some bad news for these up standing gentlemen. The lawyer explained that because they made the threat, they had better hope that neither machine stopped producing. These men thought better of carrying out their threat.

The mill did fly the flag at half staff. The men did not carry out their threat of sabotaging the paper machines. But flying the flag at half staff to honor Dr. Martin Luther King, Jr. must have been too much for some of the upstanding men of the Paper Mill Plantation to take. Being a veteran makes what someone did to our flag especially repugnant. **THEY CUT THE FLAG DOWN AND LEFT IT ON THE GROUND!**

I ached for what I knew some of the early employees had to endure at our mill. I learned most of the stories as I waged a crusade to have the Dr. Martin Luther King, Jr. holiday remain as an excused absence at our mill. I learned these stories during private conversations with some of the blacks who had been at the mill for decades.

One, now late African American employee had to suffer a number of humiliating moments. He died from cancer as did a number of other mill employees. The short time I knew him, I found him to be a knowledgeable hard worker. He was a lean muscular dark skin proud black man. He was only about ten years older than me.

I never asked him about his humiliation. I believed the person who told me about the incident. I felt their pain when he told me about the ordeal. This senior worker explained that one of the supervisors told this proud African American man to do something to embarrass him and all the black people on the floor. Both machines were running extremely well. All workers, black and white were sitting around watching the machines run. This white supervisor made this lean chocolate colored African American put a chair in the center aisle and walk around when it he had nothing else to do. **"Shades of Willie Lynch"**

Based on the experiences I have had, I believe this incident was racially motivated. However, this incident, as well as many others is accepted or should I say tolerated by all races and genders. The races and both genders for the most part are conditioned to believe that these and other demeaning acts are within the way things should be.

I recall a time during day shift, a coworker and I were working #16 Reel Drum. I was the Seventh Hand. The supervisor, called me on the intercom. He told me that he wanted me to go down stairs and cut down broke. I explained that I was the Seventh Hand. I said that I would send the Eight Hand (who was white). He explained, NO, I want you to go down between turn ups and cut down broke.

I could have filed a grievance. But I did not. To cut down broke in the basement involved the following; Rolls of class-4 paper/rejected paper were cut down by using a guillotine and sent back into the system by way of a large slat conveyor belt that dumped into the guillotine hydropulper to be turned into pulp to make paper. These rolls of paper had defects that prevented them from being sold. So they were sent down the lowrater to the Finishing Department. Instead of these rolls being shipped out for sale, they were held in storage to be returned to the paper making system.

These rolls of paper can range in size from small to large. The small rolls could weigh about five hundred pounds. The large rolls could weigh in excess of twelve thousands pounds. Finishing Department workers used their clamp trucks to lay down rolls in line in front of the lift trough to the guillotine conveyor.

The lift trough is a half circle open metal bin that rotates up and down by way of hydraulics. The trough is about ten feet wide with a six foot radius. The way the trough is designed is so that the opening edge is slightly lower than the floor when it is in the down position. The person cutting down the rolls pushes a roll into the trough by hand. Then they go up the stairs to the operating platform which is about four feet above the floor. The platform floor is at the same height as the guillotine conveyor. The controls for the guillotine, guillotine conveyors and the slat conveyor that dumps into the twenty foot high hydropulper are accessible from this platform.

The rolls are cut to make it easier for the hydropulper to turn the paper back to pulp. The cores are removed because cores would contaminate the paper making process. To cut down broke, the operator had to roll a roll of paper into the trough. Then they would have to go back up the stairs to the operating platform. They would then cause the trough to lift the roll of paper until it rolled out onto the south guillotine conveyor belt. There is a conveyor on either side (north and south) of the guillotine that can operate independent of each other or operate in concert. Whenever the guillotine was coming down both these conveyors stopped automatically. The guillotine conveyors were the same size, about ten feet wide east to west by twelve feet long north to south. The guillotine is approximately ten feet wide. It opens about nine feet vertically mounted on hydraulic cylinders to each side east and west.

With a roll in the trough the operator pushed the button to raise the trough. When the trough rotates far enough toward the vertical the roll of paper gently rolls out on the south guillotine conveyor. The south conveyor is engaged by the operator and moves north. The paper roll is carried north by the south conveyor and rolls into the channel located under the guillotine. If the paper does not make it into the guillotine channel, the operator turns off all systems (guillotine and all conveyors) and puts on a safety belt that is tied by lanyard to the platform. They then step on the south conveyor and nudge the roll in the channel under the guillotine.

After the roll is under the guillotine, the operator goes back to the operating platform, turns the system back on, then pushes the button that causes the paper to be cut with the guillotine. It takes two hands to make the guillotine come down. There are two buttons sufficiently far enough apart so that two hands have to be used to mash them. If either hand comes off either button the guillotine has to go back to the top, start position and reset before the cut can be completed.

After the guillotine has cut through the roll of paper, the operator turns off the system, puts on their safety belt, and goes on the conveyor belt and removes the two halves of the core and throw the halves into a nearby portable dumpster. Prior to loading the paper in the trough the plugs (flat pressed particle board disc from four inches to twelve inches depending on the inside diameter of the core and about 1.5 inches thick) are removed from each end the core. The plugs keep the core from collapsing. After the core (hard cardboard cylinder around which the paper is wound) halves are removed the operator goes to the platform. They then turn the system on automatic. As soon as the guillotine gets back to the top, the conveyor systems start. The paper is carried north. The paper is carried from the south guillotine conveyor to the north guillotine conveyor. The north guillotine conveyor carries the paper to the large slat conveyor that is on about a 30 degree incline. The south end of this conveyor is located just north and about two feet below the north end of the north guillotine conveyor. The north end of the slat conveyor rises from about two feet above the floor at its south end to about twenty two feet above the floor at the north end and dumps into the twenty foot high guillotine hydropulper.

Between turn ups (completed reels of paper being ejected) I had to go down in the basement and cut down broke. A black man who worked in the store room came by when I was doing this job. He must have sensed that I was angry. Because he asked me what was wrong. I explained the situation to him. He listen for a few minutes and said; "These c—kers will do anything". I stopped him. I explained to him that my grandfather was born around 1860 and my father was born in 1911 and I never heard either of them make a racial slur. I went on to say that if they went through what I knew they had to go through and did not make a racial slur I did not have the right to make a racial slur. Just because I did not use racial slurs, did not mean I did not recognize racism.

I do not know if he understood my position. I thought I would get back with him at a later date and have a discussion. Unfortunately, shortly after our brief exchange, he died. I do not know the circumstances surrounding his death. I know he was well liked and missed.

I still hold to the belief that I do not have the right to wallow in the after math of racist attacks which are directed at me. I will not respond in kind when someone attacks me purely based on my race. I am not sure it was racism that motivated my supervisor to send me down in the basement alone instead of the eighth hand, which was white and had less seniority than me. It could have been because I had more experience. Although it made me angry, it also made me think. After I cooled off, I gave my supervisor the benefit of the doubt. After several times between turn ups I guess I had cut down enough broke. He told me I could stop.

Because of so many blatant racist acts, some innocent acts were suspect. So I took the position that I would always try to think the best of a situation. However, some situations and stories shared made this difficult. Some of the things that happened at the mill were a reflection of the times and the **"Old South".**

In the fifties and sixties the blacks were segregated from the whites at the mill. One senior African American man was stung with anger when he told me about the situation when a supervisor ran him away from a water fountain which was reserved for whites. I played football with this supervisor's son in high school. I worked for him on the Paper Machine before he retired. I would go by to visit him at home. I thought he was a friend. I still believe he is a friend within the framework of the **"Old South"** relations.

There are a number of other examples that could be sited about race relationships at the mill. It seems that all races thought that business as usual was the way things should be. I asked a black worker who had over forty years seniority if he had ever witnessed any racial discrimination. He said no. I was dumb founded. I asked if in all the time he had been working at the mill did he know of any racist acts. He said no and moved away as if he no longer wanted to talk to me.

Many blacks would complain in their groups in front of other blacks. However, it was very rare for blacks to complain in mixed race company. Even when they did complain it seemed as though they were looking over their shoulders to make sure the wrong person did not hear them. It seemed that the racial lines were well defined.

Blacks and whites joked together. On the surface everything seemed fine. Things stayed that way as long as no one challenged the status quo. The work place environment was a reflection of the local community which held to the practices of the **"Old South"**.

I vividly remember an experience I had at the local grocery store. This grocery store is located on property owned by the Mill just off NC Highway 88N and the main road, leading to the mill. I had been working at the mill for about three years. As I often did, I stopped by this grocery store on my way home to pick up a few things.

One day when I entered the store I noticed an elderly black lady, about seventy years old, and a young white lady, about thirty years old, leaving the store as I entered. I heard the black lady tell the white lady, yes mam, similar to the way a southern child would respond to an adult. It was as if I had been transported back to the fifties. I paused long enough to get over the psychological punch in my gut. I bought my groceries and drove the twelve or so miles home. This incident, along with others, continues to weigh on me.

Even though the atmosphere at work and in the community seemed to be racist, most of the people in the area act as if the situation is normal.

Two brothers that work on the Paper Machine are good examples of this fact. I count them both as my friends. This is in spite of the fact that they were raised in a racist environment. Their father was a supervisor at the mill. He had retired before I came to work there. According to one brother, their grandfather was so racist that they were not allowed to watch a black person on television. They acknowledged that they were both raised in a racist atmosphere. However, they both seemed to overcome much of their programming.

They both worked on the Paper Machine on the same shift with me. So, we had a number of opportunities to talk. It was refreshing to talk to them. Cletus is about two years older than Rick. I am about five years older than Cletus. They both started work at the mill right out of high school.

They acknowledged the depth of the racism from which they were spawned. The racism was generational. Rick explained that on more than one occasion that he had come a long way. During one conversation, Cletus explained how he got violently angry when he saw a black and white mixed couple.

Rick had problems overcoming the encoding he had endured as a child. He was a sensitive man that wanted more than anything to do the right thing. Later, we had a discussion about the Dr. Martin Luther King, Jr. Holiday. He could not honestly see the significance of the day or much of the Civil Rights movement. We went back and forth over the merits of getting rid of segregation and other civil rights accomplishments.

Rick could not see the worth. His pure honesty motivated me to get him to see my position. After a number of conversations on the subject over several shifts I believe we found some common ground. I think Rick understood why I took exception to him wanting me to address his wife as Miss in a way similar to the elderly black woman at grocery store did to the young white woman.

After getting past this issue, we came with open minds to the topic of the civil rights movement. Part of that discussion included the importance of the Dr. Martin Luther King, Jr. birthday holiday. I explained that this holiday was a symbol of an entire race of people being recognized as equal citizens. I further explained that Dr. King worked for equality for all people regardless of race or gender. Rick was leaning but still no sale. Finally, I explained that if not for the work of Dr. King and the Civil Rights movement he and I probably would not be friends. Rick saw and accepted my position.

Cletus was equally as difficult to enlighten. I do not think he ever got over or ever will get over his distain for the mixing of the races romantically. However, I believe the events surrounding a party he threw at his home opened him up to the mingling of the races after he got over the sting.

One year, during the Christmas holidays, Cletus and his wife invited all the Paper Machine crews to their home for a party. They made preparations for a large gathering. Cletus and his wife were gracious hosts. Cletus was noticeably hurt and angered by the light turn out. Only four people showed up for their party. Amos and his wife, a white couple and my wife and I were the only guest. Cletus seemed grateful that we showed up. He seemed determined never to do it again.

I think Cletus was reminded that there are jerks in both races. He also learned that there are people that are OK in both races. I was glad that we could witness this evolution. But like many others in the community and in the mill there was a long way to go to reach completion of the evolution. Cletus and Rick, along with some others at our mill might be evolving.

The mill and the community seemed to be evolving. But there was and is a foot in the past. There is the case of Ronald that linked the buffoonery of the **"Old South"** to a slowed evolutionary process. To my astonishment and the amusement of many on the operating floor Ronald imitated the antics of an orangutan. When the mood hit him, Ronald would walk the aisle mimicking Clint Eastwood's costar Clyde the orangutan. I have to admit that with his beard, long hair, facial expressions and apparent double jointed body he was a dead ringer for Clyde.

The mood to put on a show usually coincided with visitors coming to the operating floor. Some of the people on the floor almost died from laughter. Others almost died from shame as he put on his show. On the surface it may have looked like good fun. But when one looks below the surface, one sees that the activity was demeaning, confirming the thoughts of many that we blacks were near relatives to the monkey.

If this wasn't enough, there were occasional shows that were put on, that conjured up memories of the group that targeted blacks. A few black men left themselves opened to be sexually assaulted. A white man would come up behind a willing black man and slap him between the legs from behind on his genitals. The black man would dance around as if he were trying to get away but to no avail. The usual expression on the black man's face indicated that he was a willing participant. These frequent shows were met by roars of laughter by most of the white audience and some of the blacks.

The roars of laughter were like an ice pick in my heart. I wondered if those participating in these distasteful acts remembered or was reliving what would happen to black men in the **"Old South"** if he were accused by a white woman of being disrespectful. I learned what the consequences were for a black man being accused of being inappropriate by a white woman from a white classmate when I was in the eighth grade, the first year I attended an integrated school.

Jack seemed to be a friendly guy. We became friends. As a matter of fact we are still friends today. After we got to know each other a little better we would talk. I believe I was an enigma to Jack. I believe he thought I was strange because I did not accept the scientific notion he shared that whites were naturally more intelligent than blacks. He would site different studies I believe he was taught by the adults in his life to prove his point.

When I did not accept Jack's propaganda about white superior intellect, he shared other information he thought I should know. The most information he shared was about the retribution of white men against black men who were accused of being disrespectful to a white woman. One type of retribution was if a white woman accused a black man of being inappropriate with her, was for a group of the upstanding white men to put the black man in an out house/toilet. These white men would saturate the toilet with gasoline. They would then throw a knife or razor in with the black man. They would then tell the black man to send out his genitals or they would burn the toilet with him in it. I do not think I showed any emotion. I knew this story and worst stories were true. But, why do I have to relive this holocaust at the place where I am employed?

There is a written set of rules which is our corporate blue print to a wonderful harmonious work environment. Every year each employee has to complete a course administered on the computer to ensure we are safety conscience and current with the latest procedures to do certain jobs safely. Included in this computer course is a section dedicated to the fair treatment of all employees. This section is called Respect and Dignity.

In principle this training is outstanding. However, in practice at our Mill it falls short. During the quarter in which an employee's birth month falls, the employee is required to complete a number of training modules. This training loses its credibility because an answer key can be had for the asking from ones supervisor. The fact that employees do these modules for other employees further diminishes the credibility of this training.

Our employer has to know something about the bottom line to have become the largest paper producer of the kinds of paper it produces in the world. This fact is commendable. It appears that the personnel/production balance is a condition that our employer has learned how to maintain in over one hundred years of its existence. I am sure it has to be a logistical nightmare to coordinate the interests that are controlled by our employer all over the planet. Overall it appears that they take all aspects of its business operations serious.

During the course of the challenges I have faced at the Mill, I talked to a number of people to resolve the issues. I talked to members of supervision, Human Resources at the Mill and at corporate level. I believe I exhausted every channel available to me. Corporate even sent Ms. Jackie, Human Resources, Pensacola Florida Mill to meet with me at our Mill. I had a conversation with each of the Mill Managers during my employment about the issues of racism and unfair treatment.

On November 24, 2011 at 11:50 am I was frozen in time. Something happened that had a tremendous impact on my life. Frank brought me a flyer sent by my supervisor. I have heard that just before a person dies their entire life flashes before their eyes. When Frank came to me, it seemed as if my work life at our Mill flashed before my eyes.

I now work in maintenance. I have been on light duty/restricted duty since July 2010. Fast forwarding through the rejections for advancement I experienced while working in production on the Paper Machine brings me to being escorted by my maintenance supervisor to a small office just outside of the Mill gate in the Administrative Building.

In a few minutes I relived escorting the IP "COACH" Lee around our Mill. I will remember the comment he made about one of his former players during his speech and magic trick after his tour. He said to an audience of Mill employees, referring to me, he is as tall lying down as he is standing up. Unfortunately that speech was videoed. So, even if everyone forgot that infamous comment, the video will always be around to remind them.

I got to escort my former college football coach because I asked the Mill Manager. I was one of the lesser members of the committee that coordinated the visit. Rick, another member of the committee made it clear he was not impressed with me escorting the Coach. Our employer was pushing the team concept for the corporation. Even though I had gained over one hundred pounds in the twenty plus years since I played football, I thought I would test to see if he really remembered me.

We were riding the golf cart alone to different departments when I posed some questions to him. I asked if he remembered Jude Stokes. I believe, to be kind, he indicated that he remembered Jude. Before he remembered too much, I pointed out to him that Jude didn't come to State until after he had left to go coach in the National Football League. I went on to thank him. I told him I didn't care if he remembered me or not. I was riding in a golf cart away from hard work. This day I was getting over like a fat rat. I wonder if the comment about me being taller lying down than standing up in is farewell speech had anything to do with our alone time conversation.

When the coach left, I thought my stock at the Mill had risen. I was wrong. The few opportunities I thought were available for someone like me had become less. However, I could still progress along the lines of seniority. While I was doing all I could do to get ahead, I was still trying to find other challenges. Maintenance was a better option. The pay was better and the hours were straight days with every weekend off.

More money, better working conditions (scheduled lunches and breaks) and better working hours made maintenance a no brainer. However, moving from production to maintenance was not an easy task. Around 1998 all employees were given a chance through the Maintenance Apprenticeship Program (MAP) to get into maintenance, or so we thought. We were told that the only way we would be considered for maintenance was to complete a number of courses taught by instructors sanctioned by the local community college and taught at our Mill. We had to complete the work on our own time and receive no pay for our efforts. Approximately eighty production personnel started the 756 hour program. Only nine of us completed the program.

During the last few weeks of the program, rumors started flying. It was being said that our union had not sanctioned the MAP program. So, completing MAP would have no bearing on whether someone would be considered for maintenance. The nine of us left in the program asked for a meeting with the head of HR and our union president. During this meeting, they promised that going through the Maintenance Apprenticeship Program was the only way to get into maintenance.

After this meeting we continued to go through the program. I attended the minimum amount of time that would still allow me to get a certificate of completion. Something just did not feel right. I wrote a letter to the head of HR, and our union president, thanking them and repeating what they had promised us. Each of the nine remaining members of the program signed the letter. One of the white signees asked me who helped me write the letter.

Our HR director and Union President responded to our letter within a couple of days. They each made clarifications that rendered their promises worthless. Another meeting followed. Their lies corrected their mistakes. The union meeting that followed and many conversations gave us nine no leverage for getting into maintenance.

We had about two weeks to finish the program. Seven of the nine in MAP were from the Paper Machine. I went along with the group as it was decided that we were going to finish the program no matter what the union did. We finished. The union voted against the Map Program in favor of an apprenticeship program they and the company endorsed.

The company agreed to pay the participants for their time. There would be a number of groups containing twelve employees each that would cycle through the local community college's on campus classes. Each apprentice would get an associate's degree. The company paid for books, travel, time and all fees.

In order to get in this new apprenticeship program, employees had to pass a test. Then they would be selected by seniority. A few days before the program was started, I was called at home by the HR secretary. She explained to me that I could not take the test to be considered for the apprenticeship program because I had too many absences. I explained that I had never had an oral or written reprimand for having too many absences. My comments did not seem to faze her as she held to her position that I would not be able to take the test.

I felt like I was in the twilight zone. Before she hung up I asked her a few questions. How many absences did I have that made it too many for me to take the test to be considered for the Apprenticeship Program? The secretary explained that she could not answer that question. By now, it seemed as though Rod Serling was whispering in my ear from the "Twilight Zone". I asked the secretary what was the system used to determine that I had too many absences. She said I can't answer that. To be clear, I said; do you mean to tell me that I have too many absences but you cannot tell me how many too many I have or how it was determined that I had too many. After a brief silence . . . . I heard, I can't answer that.

Armed with this rejection, I went to our new Mill Manager. I explained the situation. He explained to me that he would look into the matter. The next day I got a call at home. I was told I could take the test to see if I would be considered for the Apprenticeship Program. A few days after taking the test I got a call at home. I was told that I passed the test. But there were only twelve slots available and I was number thirteen. They further explained that the only way I could get in the program was that one of the people already accepted would have to drop out. Sure enough, two people decided not to participate. I and one other person were allowed to participate in the program.

I was grateful for this turn of events. But I was mystified to hear from coworkers that I was the only black to pass the qualifying test. It makes me wonder.

After a number of disturbing events on my way to completing the Apprenticeship Program, I wound up working in the #16 Paper Machine Maintenance Shop. The only permanent black first line maintenance supervisor at the mill was my supervisor. About a year after my arrival, he was transferred to another maintenance shop. That left the #16 Maintenance Supervisor slot vacant. I tried to apply for the position. I was told by HR that they were not going to fill this position. However, up until about two years ago, a white man held this position and made my life a living hell.

About two years ago one of the transfers from the Mill that closed in Natchez, was given this **"NONPOSITION"**. I was told that he was handpicked for the position. He had been a Mill Right maintenance shift worker. An African American was an electrician maintenance shift worker on the same shift as he. Shortly before he was promoted to supervisor he had several verbal and a physical confrontation with this African American, according to the African American. According to this African American, the man from Natchez would use racial slurs in an attempt to intimidate him. The Electrical and Instrumentation maintenance workers are called "Neck Ups". Mechanical Maintenance workers are called "Neck Downs". This African American man explained that he had complained to Human Resources about the man from Natchez. After the physical confrontation he explained that the man from Natchez was sent to anger management.

This African American man was the chairman of the Mill's Benefit Association Board. I was a volunteer board member. The function of the Benefit Association Board was to oversee the running of the cafeteria and the vending machines. The profits from these services are used to benefit the workers that are members of the Association. This African American man shared with me his confrontations and frustrations with the man from Natchez. When he was still on shift, this man from Natchez said to me "I thought you were prejudice. But I see you are not because you took Robert E. Lee's birthday off too". This comment was made after I returned to work after an extended vacation around the time of Dr. Martin Luther King, Jr. Birthday Holiday Celebration. This man from Natchez was in our shop area when he made the observation. Most of the people in the shop, by their reaction, seemed to think his little joke was funny.

This man from Natchez is the supervisor for #16 Paper Machine Maintenance crew. Since he has been my supervisor, I have had other opportunities to sample his sense of humor. Sending Frank to bring me the flyer about the danger of lead in the drinking water at the mill reminds me of how things used to be in the **"Old South"**. The house Negro brought something to the field Negro for the Master. Frank threatened me after I spoke up against the supervisor slapping him up between his legs from behind on his genitals while he danced a jig to the laughter and delight of others in our break room.

The day before a similar show had been performed. I was mortified. But I did not say anything. I got Frank by himself and explained to him how offensive I thought the emasculating display was to me. Frank seemed to be in agreement. So, I decided at my earliest opportunity I would try and reason with our boss man to get this behavior stopped.

But as fortune would have it, I did not get a chance to speak to him that day. Before I could speak to him alone the following day, they were replaying the drama for the crew to laugh while some of us died inside. This act occurred the following morning as we were getting our work assignments for the day. When I saw Frank lean over the boss' desk with the boss behind him with a fly swatter, I hoped for the best. But I saw the worst.

The boss tapped Frank repeatedly from behind between his legs on his private area. Frank seemed to be enjoying the assault as he danced to the delight and laughter of some of our coworkers. Before I knew it I heard myself say with a loud voice **"HOLD-UP! THAT OFFENDS ME!"** The deer in the headlights stare I got from the boss and Frank let me know that they did not have a problem with what was happening. At this point the rest of the crew left the break room as I asked the boss if I could speak to him in his office.

As we sat in the office I grappled with how to approach this situation. I probably said a prayer asking for the right words as is my custom. After a short pause, I started. I began by trying to explain how offended I was by his action. The boss reared back in his chair, folded his arms across his stomach and said with a smirk, *"I didn't touch you so you ought not to worry about it."*

It appeared I was getting nowhere fast. So, I tried a different approach. I told the story of the black being sent in the outhouse with a razor and told to send out his testicle because of an accusation made by a white woman. The story did not seem to surprise or affect the boss. I was trying to make the point of how emasculating his actions were. This approach had no effect.

I then reminded him of the challenges Frank was facing in his life. I had heard that Frank had a grandson that was seriously ill and a son that was in prison. I tried to share what I believed was the psychological pressures Frank was enduring. The boss" response to that was *"You ain't no psychiatrist."* Realizing I was not getting anywhere, I agreed and explained I was going to file a grievance as I got up to leave his office.

I left the office with the boss behind me. I was going to prepare for work while the boss went over and talked to Frank. Shortly after the boss talked to Frank, Frank approached me. Frank asked me to step back in the boss' office with him. I did. As soon as we got in the office Frank started to explain. He began by saying you can file a grievance about him messing you out of your overtime. But you better not file a grievance about what happen to me. He went on to say, if you do I better not see you away from this mill. After he finished his speech, Frank left and went out into our shop area.

I sit there for a few moments paralyzed. It was as if my brain had been scrambled. As I write this I am reminded of the house slave verses the field slave. I gathered my composer and headed out the office to speak to Frank.

The few feet I had to travel gave time for the realization that I had been threatened to sink in.

I went to Frank and stated the obvious. I explained to Frank that I did not like the fact that he threatened me. I went on to say to Frank **"YOU CAN SEE ME AT YOUR HOUSE AT THE STORE . . . YOU CAN SEE ME ANYWHERE . . . . BUT YOU DON'T THREATEN ME"**. I left him with the understanding that I would be filing a grievance concerning the incident, which I did.

The administration did not seem to be offended by the drama that was put on by the boss and Frank. But why would they be? Other workers were putting on the same show throughout the mill. However, they did do something about this incident. They answered my grievance and explained that they talked to the boss and he said he would not do it anymore. **CASE CLOSED.**

The mill grapevine carried the word around the mill like a windblown brush fire. It seemed that because of me, a fun part of the work environment had to be halted or at least in my presence it did not happen. Very often I would hear people say in a loud voice **THAT OFFENDS ME.** It seemed to be for my benefit even though the comments were supposed to be directed at someone else. I was told on a number of occasions by coworkers that a thing I was doing offended them. I would usually apologize. But it got to be so ridiculous that I would just laugh.

I thought my actions would benefit everyone. My hope was that we could get pass the social differences and treat each other with respect and dignity. This was not to be. Some behaviors and attitudes die hard. For this and other stands I had taken I had become an outcast.

As I was walking toward our cafeteria, I met an African American coworker friend. As is our custom, I offered my right hand for a hand shake as part of our normal greeting. He rebuffed my greeting by explaining; *"I can't shake your hand in public. Someone might see me."* We both laughed. But the point was made.

I thank God for His grace and mercy that keeps me. Sometimes I lose my happiness. But because of Him, my joy is constant. Because of Him, I don't ever have to be lonely. He will never leave me or forsake me. Because of Him, I can smile when circumstance suggest I should cry. Because of Him, I know I will live even after I die. Because of Him all the weapons formed against me will not prosper. Because of Him, I **CAN** face tomorrow.

After I volunteered to be the Shop Stewart for our shop, Frank spoke against me and voted against me. When I volunteered to be the safety advocate for my shop, Frank actively saw to it that the boss who was now a part of our regular work crew, who had been dethroned by the man from Natchez, would hold the position. The memories are flooding back. It saddens me to think of the other two blacks in our shop besides myself as house Negros. I believe they have been conditioned to be the way they are.

Although the other Negro is not a union member, he nominated the boss for Safety Advocate at Frank's urging. At best the vote should have been a tie because the other Negro was not qualified to vote. However, the boss won by one vote and I accepted it. The two other white people in our shop voted for me. I guess I was getting out of my place and that made the house Negroes uncomfortable.

After all this happened, the threats, the vote and the many jokes, Frank asked me for a favor. I said sure. He asked me to do his CBTs. I said yes and I did them. I have time on my hand out here. I can't blame the house Negroes or any of the other workers who have the disease. The same disease affects people in different ways. It causes some to feel superior. It causes others to feel inferior.

When a patient becomes ill, they are not blamed for their disease as a cure is sought. I believe racism is a disease. It seems that the strand that came from Mississippi is a lot more resistant than the strand we had been combating.

I thank God for giving me a chance to share some of what is happening all over the world in different forms. To God be the glory if what is shared here will allow a healing process to begin against the disease of racism. If you are part of the human race, look at both sides of the coin and see which side you agree, if either? I come to you from within the confines of Christian faith. It is an aspect of spiritual warfare when a person dislikes another person based solely on their race. Further, if a person is liked or disliked for any other reason than the content of their character there is a problem. This idea represents a change in the order of things. People are resistant to change.

The events of July 2010 have caused me to be where I am now. I am metaphorically sitting on a time bomb and the timer is winding down. The clock started ticking when I was first hired. The alarm was set in July 2010. I hope I finish writing this before the alarm goes off and I am kicked off the Paper Mill plantation.

I injured my back July 2010 while building rolls along with two coworkers. Building rolls involves checking bearings on each end of a steel roll. Then one drags a bearing housing to each end of the roll. The housing is lifted until it lines up to go over the bearing using rigging that gives a mechanical lifting advantage. Up until I hurt my back, the normal practice was that the heavy bearing housings were dragged across the floor by hand with a strap or piece of rope to each end on the roll. Since I hurt my back, the procedure has been changed so a forklift is now used to move the housings.

Friday afternoon, July 23, 2010, while dragging a bearing housing across the floor with a nylon strap I felt a snap in my lower back followed by a white hot heat down my right leg. The sensation lasted for a few moments. It was close to 3:30pm, time to go home from work. I went home with a number of thoughts running through my head.

After taking pain pills, I thought about my injury at work in 2004. Shortly before finishing up the on sight portion of the Apprenticeship Program I got injured. We apprentices had to spend time working in the maintenance shops of each area of the mill. At the time I got my lung injury I was assigned to the back of the mill in the Digester Area (smelliest part of the mill).

One Friday evening a few of us were offered overtime to work on a Lime Harper. The Lime Harper is a large vibrating rectangular shaped funnel. We worked on the Harper while it was still running. Apparently it was necessary for this Harper to keep running in order not to interrupt production.

We all breathed in a lot of lime dust. Apparently my constitution was not as strong as the rest. God is good. The next day my older brother and I went to the hospital. We went to visit our first cousin who was in intensive care. We could not see her right away. I was not feeling well so I told my brother I was going to find a doctor to check me out.

I went to the emergency room to get checked out. The doctor that checked my breathing admitted me. I didn't get to see my cousin. As time past, I started to feel worse. They kept me over the weekend. The drugs and breathing treatments given to me at the hospital made me feel better for a time.

Monday morning I went to Health Services at work. I was told to go and see the company doctor. After my examination, the doctor explained that I needed to be in a clean air environment. I went back to Health Services at work. I told the nurses what the doctor said. I was sent to the double wide training trailer located next to the building that housed Health Services. Trainers had offices in this building. They gave me a small office to spend my time. I was there only a short time when I got word to relocate to the foreman's old office in the Bleach Plant. I did not understand why. I just did as I was told. I walked about two hundred yards toward the bowels of the mill to the office. The setup/temporary foreman was in the office. He was the supervisor during the regular foreman's absence. I arrived at the office a little after 8am. As I took inventory of the condition of the filthy office and the hint of chlorine gas that had a constant presence in the Bleach Plant, my confusion grew. I shared what had transpired with my friend, the setup foreman. I was six feet two inches tall and weighed over 300 pounds. He at about six feet seven inches tall was the only person at the mill that called me "Little Buddy".

While I was talking to him, he was doing something on the computer. I believe what happened next was divine intervention. He mentioned the company's help line phone number. I called the number. The person I was told I needed to speak to; Workman's Compensation Representative was not available. The person that answered the phone gave me their cell number.

I dialed the number. She answered my call as she was getting out of her car along with her boss in the parking lot of our Mill. I gave her a synopsis of my situation. She explained that they were at the Mill for a meeting. I asked if she could come see me after her meeting. She explained that their meeting should be over about 10:00am. I told her that anyone could direct her to the office to which I had been assigned.

At about 10:05am there came a knocking at the door. It was her, her supervisor and a procession. The company doctor, my friend's boss, company safety director, and a few others.

She seemed to be a bit miffed as she entered the office. She asked if I wanted to speak to her alone. I indicated that I did not care if they stayed. Before we started talking my friend's boss said in a nervous voice "You don't need me do you, as he backed out of the office and disappeared?"

She asked what the problem was. I looked around the dirty and dusty office in a slow exaggerated fashion. I looked at the doctor as I commented; didn't you tell me to stay in a clean environment? The company doctor stammered as he explained, all I can do is give a recommendation. It is up to the company whether they will do it or not. All eyes fell on the safety director.

The Safety Director said in a special tone, we will get him out of here soon. Then she explained that she wanted to speak to me alone. After everyone else left the office she asked me how I knew that they were in the parking lot when I called. It was just the goodness of God.

She said she thought that she was being set up. If I had waited a few minutes more I would not have gotten her because she would have turned off her phone before she went to her meeting. I thank God for the way He blesses. She explained that she would talk to me later as she left to join those that had left before her.

At about 1:30pm the Assistant Maintenance Superintendant, came by the office and told me that I was to go back to the training trailer. True to her word, the little red head woman, as she called herself, came by to talk to me before she left to go back to her office in Salisbury, North Carolina. She came to the training trailer and explained about her lunch meeting. She said that while everyone else was eating lunch they seemed to have forgotten about her.

She said she asked the Safety Director if they had gotten me out of that office. He said no. But they would be getting me out soon. She said she told him that she would go get me out of the office since she wasn't getting anything to eat. She said he then sent word for me to move back to the training trailer.

In a few days, she arranged for me to see the best pulmonary specialist in the state. He had the last word on all industrial pulmonary injuries in North Carolina. Although he taught and set on the board of directors at other hospitals, I saw him at UNC-Chapel Hill Hospital.

During this first visit I found this doctor to be very approachable. After a thorough examination, he explained my condition. My lung injury could develop into something more serious. I had an agreement with Workman's Compensation, that I would be checked out ever year to see how I was doing.

Before I had my last visit with this doctor, the Mill chose a different company to administer the Workman's Compensation cases. The last time I went for my yearly check, I started passing out during the breathing test. The doctor explained that he thought that I was having issues with my heart. He told me I needed to have a stress test as soon as possible when I got back home.

If memory serves me correctly, the new Workman's Compensation Administrator cancelled my future yearly lung evaluations. She explained that the case for my lung injury was closed because the doctor said the problem was with my heart. God has a way of showing just how good He is.

I came home and scheduled a stress test with a cardiologist in Wilmington. I think I had a nuclear stress test on a Tuesday. Apparently I was not fit enough to take the regular physical stress test. I was assured that the chemical stress test was just as effective as the regular stress test. The result of the stress test showed that I had 35% heart function. The doctor explained that I needed to get a heart catheterization as soon as possible so he could see what going on in my heart.

A heart catheterization was scheduled for me for the following Friday. I needed more information. The doctor explained the heart catheterization to me. A long tube going up through a vein in my groin into my heart was a bit unsettling. I appreciated the doctor's candor and honesty. When I asked what the worst that could happen was, he explained, you could die. I had to consider a lot of things.

Our daughter, JJ, had taken a semester (January 2008 through May 2008) off from Winston Salem State University to intern at Disney World in Orlando, Florida. The catheterization was scheduled for the Friday I was supposed to pick her up from Disney World.

Considering the fact that I might die during the heart catheterization, I decided to make sure I saw both my children before I went through the procedure. I had the procedure scheduled for the Friday after our daughter was to return from Florida. Our son had been living in Wilmington for several years. I wanted to see my children together one more time before I died.

God works in mysterious ways. That Thursday morning before the Friday I was supposed to pick my daughter up from Disney World; I went to work as usual. Fortunately the morning before I was to leave for Florida I was in a training class at work. I arrived at the employee parking lot around 6:30am. I had thirty minutes to walk the two hundred or so yards to the conference room in the Consolidated Office Building (COB) in which I was to attend training.

As I walked across the parking lot, my left arm felt like it weighed a ton. When I got to the conference room I was feeling rotten. I explained to the instructor that I was going down the hall to Health Services to get checked out. The only person in the conference room with the instructor when I arrived was my friend from college. He and I stayed on the same floor of Tucker dorm at State College my freshman year.

He took one look at me and rose quickly from his chair to prop me up. He assisted me to Health Service. The nurse had me lie on a gurney. I told her how I was feeling. She gave me a nitroglycerin tablet. I did not get a headache and I was still hurting. She gave me four baby aspirin. By now, members of the mill emergency response team had started to arrive. Just before I was loaded on the ambulance I was given another nitroglycerine tablet. I was hurting. But I did not really get concerned until I saw the company nurse loading on the ambulance with me. The nurse never leaves the mill.

The nearby rescue squad was called for advance life savings intervention. It is located near the intersection of Highway 88 and the road to the mill. By the time we travelled the approximate one mile to the rescue squad an Intermediate Emergency Medical Technician (EMT) was ready to board the ambulance.

She got on the ambulance and immediately went to work. She got a line started on me. I don't remember all she asked or all she did. By the time we got to the Emergency Room they were ready for me. They rolled me into a small room and closed the curtain. As they were getting me hooked up to intravenous fluids my beautiful wife Dalphaine arrived. The few moments we were left alone, my wife and I prayed. After we finished a nurse came by with a pad to ask some questions.

Because of my answer there is one question I do not think I will ever forget. The nurse asked, on a scale of 1 to 10 with 10 being the greatest, how bad is your pain? At the risk of being none responsive, I told the nurse that my chest felt like an elephant had sat on my chest and farted. I guess the imagery made the point.

A doctor came by the room to give me details of the emergency heart catheterization he was going to do on me. He started to give me a laundry list of different things that may need to be done. He explained that he may find that he would have to; do a bypass, put in a stint or a number of other options.

I stopped the doctor as my wife looked on, and asked him if he was a Christian? He explained that he was a Christian. I asked him to pray. He said go ahead indicating that I should pray. While lying on the gurney with my doctor and my wife around my bed, I prayed. After I got through praying, I told the doctor that if he could not wake me when he got through not to worry about it. Everything would be alright. I told him that I did not want to know about anything he did. I went on to explain to him that I wanted him to fix anything that needed fixing while I was asleep.

Within a few minutes, I was rolled to a room with an x-ray table. They moved me from the gurney to the x-ray table. They drug me from the gurney to the x-ray/operating table. I wish I could remember the name of the wonderful doctor. But I cannot. The doctor told the crew that was working with him that "He does not what to know anything about the procedure". Those were the last words I heard from the doctor while they were doing the procedure. The next words I heard from the doctor were after the procedure. I was in my hospital room. I was awakened by the doctor, who was standing by my bed, nudging me awake with his leg. As I overcame the effects of the anesthesia, I heard him say **"we could not find any blockage"**. To God be the glory.

As soon as the doctor left a nurse came by to remove the cathode. I was not awake when it was inserted. So, I did not know what she was doing fumbling around my groin. I was just about to object when she pulled the tube out of my groin. I was relieved as she placed a bandage at the insertion spot and told me I could not move for three hours. She reminded me that the tube entered through my femoral artery. If I moved I could bleed to death. It was 3:30pm.

I lay perfectly still until 6:35pm. We rang for the nurse. When she arrived, I asked if I could go home since I had been still for over three hours. She looked at my groin and said everything looked OK. She then explained that I had to prove that I could walk around OK before I could be released from the hospital.

I closed the gown around me, put on the hospital socks and started my walk around the nurse stations. After I walked one lap, I informed the nurse. She indicated that I could go home. I said I was going to walk a victory lap.

When I finished walking my victory lap, my discharge papers were ready. I was told I could go home. I prepared to walk to the elevator. But the nurse stopped me and told me I had to ride a wheel chair out the hospital. By the time we got out the front door of the hospital; Dalphaine was waiting with the car.

God had done another wonderful thing in my life. I went home feeling better than I had felt in a long time. After a great night sleep I got up before daybreak the next morning and headed to Orlando alone to get our baby, JJ. I drove almost six hundred miles in about nine hours. I picked up our daughter and then headed back home. We arrived home Saturday morning without incident. God is so good.

Throughout my life, God has delivered me from many challenges. Delivering me from chest pains and the long drive was a matter of God continuing to be merciful and good in my life. The goodness and mercy of God is what gives me confidence and endurance in spite of all odds.

As you read this, understand that God has not blessed me because I am special. He blessed me because He is special. Every person on the planet is equally loved by God. Acts 10:34-35 [34]Then Peter opened his mouth, and said, Of a truth I perceive that God is no respecter of persons: [35]But in every nation he that feareth him, and worketh righteousness, is accepted with him.

A confidence in God is what gave me the ability to say what I did during my Third Step grievance I had at the mill. All Third Step Grievances are heard during the same time one after the other. A grievance gets to this point after the company and the person for whom the grievance has been filed have gotten to a point where outside intervention is needed to come to an agreement. At this meeting were fourteen people from all levels of management and representatives from our union. The conversation had gotten to a point where it appeared my cause was lost.

Out of exasperation and I believe divine guidance, I asked; "how many of you are Christians?" The Mill Manager started to say what does that have to do with anything? As he looked around and saw all hands up except his, he raised his hand. I took this moment to make the statement that I think back on when I am being challenged. I said; *"YOU ALL MAY BE ABLE TO BEAT ME. BUT YOU CANNOT BEAT THE GOD I SERVE"*.

I have had to rely on the truth of this comment more the last fourteen months than I have had to in my previous time at the Mill. I vividly remember sitting on a golf buggy at the #16 Roll Storage area. The now dethroned boss took exception at me watching him and others build rolls. Red faced and apparently full of anger, he gestured wildly and screamed for me to get away from there. As he moved toward me, he said; *"YOU AIN'T GOING TO SIT DOWN AND WATCH ME WORK"*.

I was in a pickle. The man from Natchez didn't want me to stay around our shop/break area. But going back to the shop was preferable to having a confrontation with angry man. So, I drove two hundred or so yards back to our shop area through the basement. Shortly after my encounter with the dethroned boss, the man from Natchez escorted me to the Administrative Building located just outside the fenced-in area of the mill.

God is so good. What they purposed for my bad turned out to be for my good. The man from Natchez escorted me to the office of the production lead safety advocate. Next to the Production Lead Safety Advocate's office is the office of the Maintenance Lead Safety Advocate. The man from Natchez explained to the Production Lead Safety Advocate that I would be out there with them to help any way they saw fit.

I was presented like a small child on their first day of school. The Production Lead Safety Advocate directed me to the smallest of the three offices. He explained that another employee had occupied this office during the almost three years he was on light duty. This office was assigned to the Women of Steel, the females of our union. They all worked together for the good of the union and company.

The position of the lead safety advocates are filled at the pleasure of the union president. They oversee a union backed, company sanctioned safety program. The program allows for and encourages employee participation. There is also a safety newsletter that is supposed to come out each month. I asked and was given an opportunity to help work on the newsletter. This was fun while it lasted.

It appears that I am nearing the end of my employment at our Mill. Therapy for my back injury was discontinued this past October. I met with the head of Human Resources alone and with my Union President on another occasion. It was explained to me by the head of Human Resources that the only job I would do at the mill is maintenance mechanic. The physical requirements of this job exceed the limitations put upon me by the doctor.

My Union President argued that I was qualified for a number of other jobs at the mill. I was an honor graduate from a four year institution. I also served as a captain in the United States Army. I finished the in class portion of the Front Line Leadership program. The discussion seemed to be going nowhere. So, I told my President that I had learned what I needed to know and we left.

During my time at the Mill, it has been thrust upon me by conscience and I hope a desire to do God's Will, the need to stand against injustices. The most glaring injustices have been and it appears will continue to be racism and discrimination.

I could go through the mind numbing details of all that has happened since I have been on light duty. However, it would be rehashing a different version of what has been going on in the "Old South" for centuries. We have come a long way as a country. However, Satan still finds fertile ground to grow his seeds of discourse. It appears he has a bumper crop at the Paper Mill Plantation. Some whites by doing and some blacks by accepting will keep our Mill part of the "Old South".

I once asked during a Third Step Grievance if the attendees knew who Willie Lynch was. Some by dropping their heads acknowledged that they did. Others asked who he was. I asked the attendees to GOOGLE Willie

Lynch and see what they found. I figured that some of them would see themselves.

This battle is not and for that matter has never been mine.

I will hold to this truth with my final breath; *"YOU MAY BE ABLE TO BEAT ME. BUT YOU CANNOT BEAT THE GOD I SERVE."*

IT WILL ONLY BE BY DIVINE INTERVENTION THAT OUR MILL, OUR HEARTS AND OUR AMERICA WILL BE HEALED.

www.ingramcontent.com/pod-product-compliance
Lightning Source LLC
Chambersburg PA
CBHW050337290526
45785CB00006B/2537